Different Teeth of Animals

by Grace Hansen

Abdo Kids Jumbo is an Imprint of Abdo Kids
abdobooks.com

abdobooks.com

Published by Abdo Kids, a division of ABDO, P.O. Box 398166, Minneapolis, Minnesota 55439.
Copyright © 2024 by Abdo Consulting Group, Inc. International copyrights reserved in all countries.
No part of this book may be reproduced in any form without written permission from the publisher.
Abdo Kids Jumbo™ is a trademark and logo of Abdo Kids.

Printed in the United States of America, North Mankato, Minnesota.

052023

092023

THIS BOOK CONTAINS
RECYCLED MATERIALS

Photo Credits: Getty Images, Shutterstock

Production Contributors: Teddy Borth, Jennie Forsberg, Grace Hansen
Design Contributors: Candice Keimig, Pakou Moua

Library of Congress Control Number: 2022946802
Publisher's Cataloging-in-Publication Data

Names: Hansen, Grace, author.

Title: Different teeth of animals / by Grace Hansen

Description: Minneapolis, Minnesota : Abdo Kids, 2024 | Series: Amazing animal features | Includes online
     resources and index.

Identifiers: ISBN 9781098266295 (lib. bdg.) | ISBN 9781098266998 (ebook) | ISBN 9781098267346
     (Read-to-me ebook)

Subjects: LCSH: Animals--Juvenile literature. | Body composition--Juvenile literature. | Teeth--Juvenile
     literature. | Zoology--Juvenile literature.

Classification: DDC 591.1--dc23

Table of Contents

Different Teeth of Animals

There are different teeth in the animal kingdom. Certain tooth shapes help animals survive!

Herbivores

Animals that only eat plants are called herbivores. They have special teeth that help them eat plants.

An herbivore's **incisor** teeth

are sharp. These teeth help

the animal tear plants such

as grass and leaves.

Some animals have **incisor** teeth on the tops and bottoms of their mouths. Others, such as sheep and goats, only have lower incisors.

The **molars** of an herbivore are wide and flat. These teeth help mash up the food. Plant matter is hard to **digest** unless it is ground up.

incisors
molars
13

Carnivores

Carnivores are animals that only eat meat. Before they can eat, they first must catch their food.

A carnivore has sharp incisor teeth and pointed canine teeth. These kinds of teeth are used for catching prey and tearing away meat. Carnivores can also have sharp molars for chewing.

17

Carnivores such as sharks
do not need **molars**. This is
because they swallow pieces of
meat whole without chewing it.

Omnivores

Omnivores are animals that eat both plants and meat. They often have **incisor**, **canine**, and **molar** teeth. This is because they eat a **variety** of foods.

21

Teeth Check!

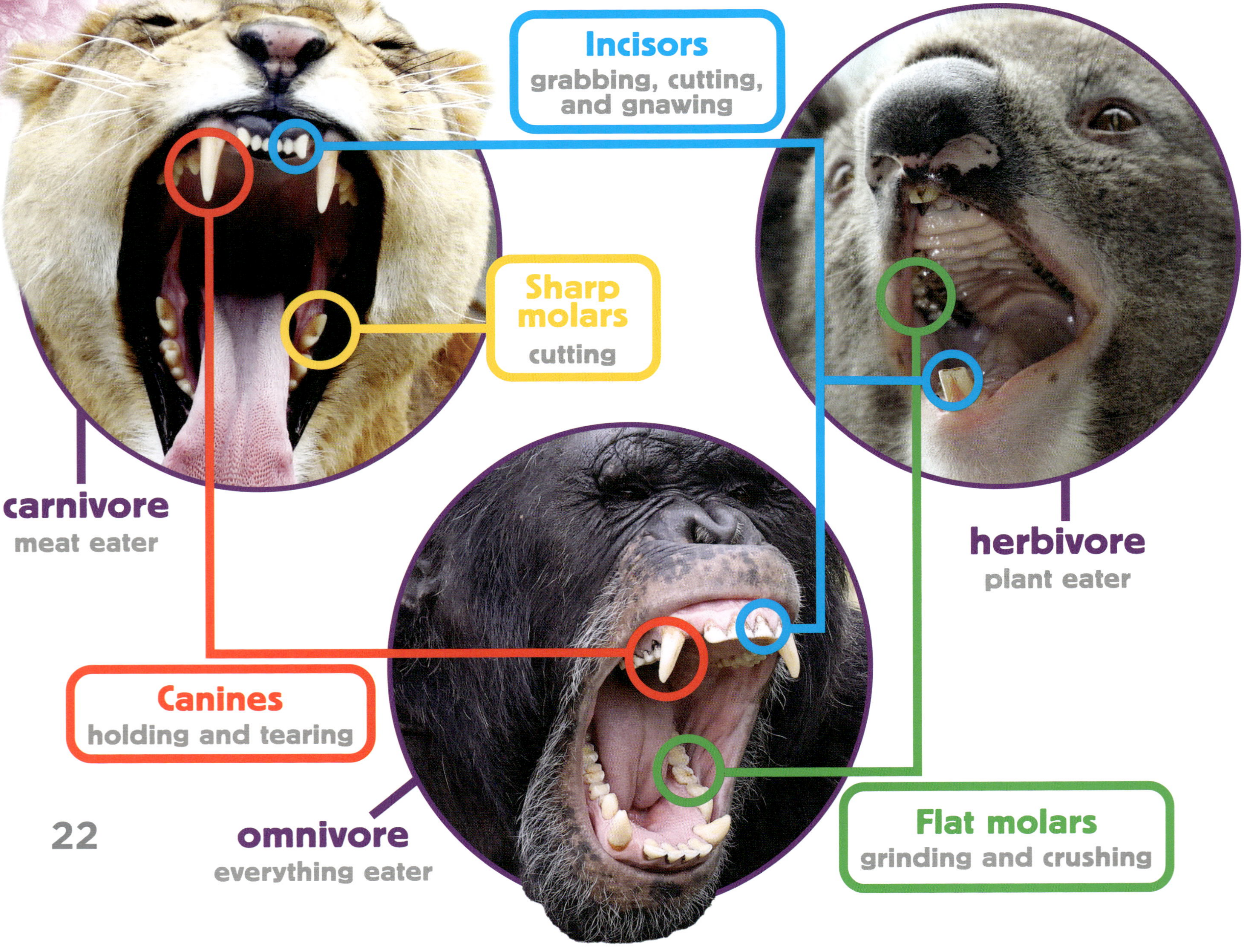
Incisors
grabbing, cutting, and gnawing
Sharp molars
cutting
carnivore
meat eater
herbivore
plant eater
Canines
holding and tearing
omnivore
everything eater
Flat molars
grinding and crushing

Glossary

canine – a pointed tooth between the front teeth and the molars of many animals.

digest – to break down materials that can be used by the body.

incisor – in mammals, one of the four sharp teeth located between the canines in each jaw at the front of the mouth.

molar – a large tooth located in the back of the mouth, with a large biting surface used for grinding food.

prey – an animal that is hunted by other animals for food.

variety – a number of different things in a group.

Index

canine teeth 16, 20

goats 10

hunting 14, 16

incisor teeth 8, 10, 16, 20

meat eating 14, 16, 18, 20

molar teeth 12, 16, 20

plant eating 6, 8, 10, 12, 20

prey 16

sharks 18

sheep 10

Visit **abdokids.com** to access crafts, games, videos, and more!